The Wild Music Book of

Christmas Carols

For Alto Saxophone with Guitar Chords

21 Tremendous Traditional

Christmas Carols

Arranged especially for Alto Saxophone
and Guitar Chord Accompaniment

With words to all the carols

Easy saxophone part

In easy keys for the saxophone player

Amanda Oosthuizen

Jemima Oosthuizen

Wild Music Publications
www.wildmusicpublications.com

We hope you enjoy *The Wild Music Book of Christmas Carols for Alto Saxophone with Guitar Chords!*

Take a look at other exciting books in the series Including: *Christmas Duets, Trick or Treat – A Halloween Suite, More Christmas Duets, 40+ Country Dances, Fun Folk for Fun Folk, Classic Duets for Intermediate players, 50+ Greatest Classics, The Flying Flute Book of Music Theory (especially for flute players), Easy Traditional Duets, Easy Tunes from Around the World,* and many more!

For more information on other amazing books please go to:
http://WildMusicPublications.com

For a **free** sample of our book of **Christmas Carols** (no need to download if you already have the book!) AND a **free play-along backing track** visit:

http://WildMusicPublications.com

Happy Tooting!

The Wild Music Publications Team

To keep up-to-date with our new releases, why not **follow us on Twitter**

@WMPublications

© Copyright 2018 Wild Music Publications

The music in this book is protected by copyright and may not be reproduced in any way for sale or private use without the consent of the author.

Contents

Away in a Manger 14

Coventry Carol 17

Deck the Halls 32

Gloucestershire Wassail 40

God Rest Ye Merry Gentlemen 12

Good King Wenceslas 4

Hark the Herald 20

In the Bleak Midwinter 34

It Came Upon a Midnight Clear 18

Jingle Bells 2

O Come All Ye Faithful 8

Once in Royal David's City 24

Past Three O'clock 26

Sans Day Carol 36

Silent Night 6

Sussex Carol 38

The First Noel 22

The Holly and the Ivy 28

We Three Kings 10

We Wish You a Merry Christmas 30

While Shepherds Watched 16

Jingle Bells

Guitar Chords
(standard tuning)

Dashing through the snow In a one-horse o-pen sleigh,

O'er the hills we go, laugh-ing all the way Bells on bob-tail

ring Ma-king spi-rits bright What fun it is to ride and sing this

Chorus

sleigh-ing song to-night OH! Jin-gle bells jin-gle bells jin-gle all the

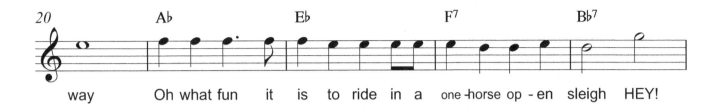

A day or two ago
I thought I'd take a ride
And soon, Miss Fanny Bright
Was seated by my side,
The horse was lean and lank
Misfortune seemed his lot
He got into a drifted bank
And then we got upsot.
[*Chorus*]

Now the ground is white
Go it while you're young,
Take the girls along
and sing this sleighing song;
Just get a bobtailed bay
Two forty as his speed
Hitch him to an open sleigh
And crack! You'll take the lead.
[*Chorus*]

A day or two ago,
The story I must tell
I went out on the snow,
And on my back I fell;
A gent was riding by
In a one-horse open sleigh,
He laughed as there I sprawling lie
But quickly drove away.
[*Chorus*]

Good King Wenceslas

Guitar Chords
(standard tuning)

Good King Wen-ces - las looked out   on the Feast of Ste - phen

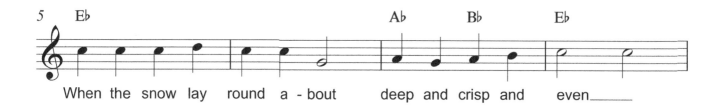

When the snow lay round a - bout   deep and crisp and even____

Bright - ly shone the moon that night   tho' the frost was cruel____

When a poor man came in sight   gath'-ring win - ter fuel____

"Hither, page, and stand by me, if thou know'st it, telling,
Yonder peasant, who is he? Where and what his dwelling?"
"Sire, he lives a good league hence, underneath the mountain;
Right against the forest fence, by Saint Agnes' fountain."

"Bring me flesh, and bring me wine, bring me pine logs hither:
Thou and I shall see him dine, when we bear them thither. "
Page and monarch, forth they went, forth they went together;
Through the rude wind's wild lament and the bitter weather.

"Sire, the night is darker now, and the wind blows stronger;
Fails my heart, I know not how; I can go no longer."
"Mark my footsteps, good my page. Tread thou in them boldly
Thou shalt find the winter's rage freeze thy blood less coldly."

In his master's steps he trod, where the snow lay dinted;
Heat was in the very sod which the saint had printed.
Therefore, Christian men, be sure, wealth or rank possessing,
Ye who now will bless the poor, shall yourselves find blessing.

Silent Night

Guitar Chords
(standard tuning)

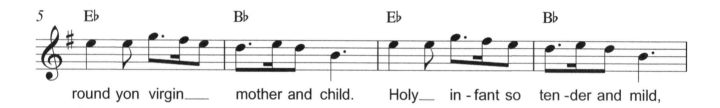

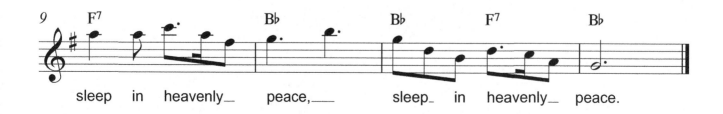

Silent night, holy night,
shepherds quake at the sight;
glories stream from heaven afar,
heavenly hosts sing Alleluia!
Christ the Savior is born,
Christ the Savior is born!

Silent night, holy night,
Son of God, love's pure light;
radiant beams from thy holy face
with the dawn of redeeming grace,
Jesus, Lord, at thy birth,
Jesus, Lord, at thy birth.

Silent night, holy night,
wondrous star, lend thy light;
with the angels let us sing,
Alleluia to our King;
Christ the Savior is born,
Christ the Savior is born!

O Come All Ye Faithful

Guitar Chords
(standard tuning)

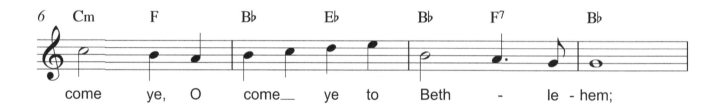

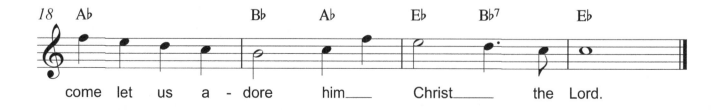

God of God, light of light,
Lo, he abhors not the Virgin's womb;
Very God, begotten, not created:
O come, let us adore Him,
O come, let us adore him,
O come, let us adore him,
Christ the Lord.

Sing, choirs of angels, sing in exultation,
Sing, all ye citizens of Heaven above!
Glory to God, glory in the highest:
O come, let us adore Him,
O come, let us adore him,
O come, let us adore him,
Christ the Lord.

Yea, Lord, we greet thee, born this happy morning;
Jesus, to thee be glory given!
Word of the Father, now in flesh appearing!
O come, let us adore Him,
O come, let us adore him,
O come, let us adore him,
Christ the Lord.

We Three Kings

Guitar Chords
(standard tuning)

We three King of Orient are; Bearing gifts we

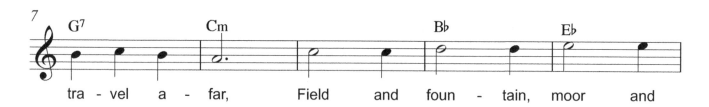

tra - vel a - far, Field and foun - tain, moor and

moun - tain, Follow - ing yon - der star.

Chorus

O___ star of won - der, star of night,

Star with royal___ beauty___ bright, West - ward lead - ing,

still pro - ceed - ing, Guide us to they per - fect light.

Born a King on Bethlehem's plain
Gold I bring to crown Him again,
King forever, ceasing never,
Over us all to reign.
[Chorus]

Frankincense to offer have I;
Incense owns a Deity nigh;
Prayer and praising, voices raising,
Worshipping God on high.
[Chorus]

Myrrh is mine, its bitter perfume
Breathes a life of gathering gloom;
Sorrowing, sighing, bleeding, dying,
Sealed in the stone cold tomb.
[Chorus]

Glorious now behold Him arise;
King and God and sacrifice;
Alleluia, Alleluia,
Peals through the earth and skies.
[Chorus]

God Rest Ye Merry Gentlemen

Guitar Chords
(standard tuning)

From God our heavenly Father
A blessed angel came,
And unto certain shepherds
Brought tidings of the same,
How that in Bethlehem was born
The Son of God by name:
[Refrain]

The shepherds at those tidings
Rejoiced much in mind,
And left their flocks a-feeding
In tempest, storm and wind,
And went to Bethlehem straightway,
This blessed Babe to find:
[Refrain]

But when to Bethlehem they came,
Whereat this Infant lay,
They found Him in a manger,
Where oxen feed on hay;
His mother Mary kneeling,
Unto the Lord did pray:
[Refrain]

Now to the Lord sing praises,
All you within this place
Like we true loving brethren,
Each other to embrace,
For the merry time of Christmas
Is coming on a-pace
[Refrain]

Away in a Manger

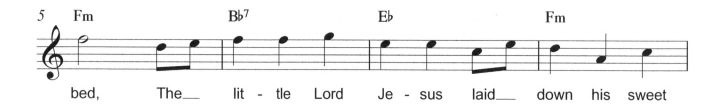

The cattle are lowing, the baby awakes
But little Lord Jesus, no crying He makes.
I love Thee, Lord Jesus, look down from the sky.
And stay by my side till morning is nigh.

The cattle are lowing the baby awakes
But little Lord Jesus no crying he makes.
I love you Lord Jesus; look down from the sky
And stay by my side until morning is nigh.

Be near me Lord Jesus I ask you to stay
Close by me for ever, and love me, I pray.
Bless all the dear children in your tender care,
And fit us for heaven, to live with you there

While Shepherds Watched

Guitar Chords
(standard tuning)

While shep-herds watchd their flocks by night, All sea-ted on the

ground, The A-ngel of the Lord came down, And glo-ry shone a-round.

"Fear not," said he for mighty dread
had seized their troubled mind
"glad tidings of great joy I bring
to you and all mankind.

"To you, in David's town, this day
is born of David's line
a Savior, who is Christ the Lord;
and this shall be the sign:

"The heavenly babe you there shall find
to human view displayed,
all simply wrapped in swaddling clothes
and in a manger laid."

Thus spoke the angel. Suddenly
appeared a shining throng
of angels praising God, who thus
addressed their joyful song:

"All glory be to God on high,
and to the earth be peace;
to those on whom his favor rests
goodwill shall never cease."

Coventry Carol

Guitar Chords
(standard tuning)

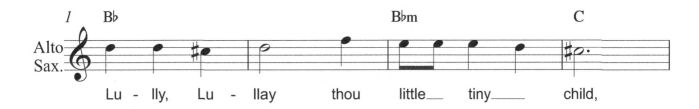

Lu - lly, Lu - llay thou little tiny child,

Bye bye, Lu - llu, Lu - llay, Lu - lly, Lu - llay, thou

little ti - ny child, Bye bye, Lu - lly, Lu - llay.

O sisters too, how may we do
For to preserve this day
This poor youngling for whom we sing,
"Bye bye, lully, lullay"

Herod the king, in his raging,
Charged he hath this day
His men of might in his own sight
All young children to slay.

That woe is me, poor child, for thee
And ever mourn and may
For thy parting neither say nor sing,
"Bye bye, lully, lullay."

It Came Upon a Midnight Clear

Guitar Chords
(standard tuning)

Still through the cloven skies they come,
With peaceful wings unfurled,
And still their heavenly music floats
O'er all the weary world;
Above its sad and lowly plains,
They bend on hovering wing,
And ever o'er its Babel sounds
The blessèd angels sing.

Yet with the woes of sin and strife
The world has suffered long;
Beneath the angel-strain have rolled
Two thousand years of wrong;
And man, at war with man, hears not
The love-song which they bring;
O hush the noise, ye men of strife,
And hear the angels sing.

And ye, beneath life's crushing load,
Whose forms are bending low,
Who toil along the climbing way
With painful steps and slow,
Look now! for glad and golden hours
come swiftly on the wing.
O rest beside the weary road,
And hear the angels sing!

For lo!, the days are hastening on,
By prophet bards foretold,
When with the ever-circling years
Comes round the age of gold
When peace shall over all the earth
Its ancient splendors fling,
And the whole world give back the song
Which now the angels sing.

Hark! The Herald Angels Sing

Guitar Chords
(standard tuning)

Refrain

Christ, by highest heaven adored,
Christ, the everlasting Lord!
Late in time behold him come,
offspring of the virgin's womb.
Veiled in flesh the Godhead see;
hail the incarnate Deity,
pleased as man with us to dwell,
Jesus, our Immanuel.
[Refrain]

Hail the heaven-born Prince of Peace!
Hail the Sun of Righteousness!
Light and life to all he brings,
risen with healing in his wings.
Mild, he lays his glory by,
born that we no more may die,
born to raise us from the earth,
born to give us second birth.
[Refrain]

The First Noel

Guitar Chords
(standard tuning)

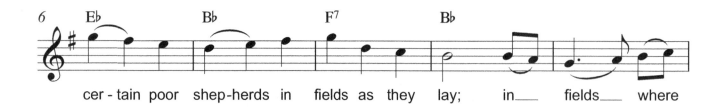

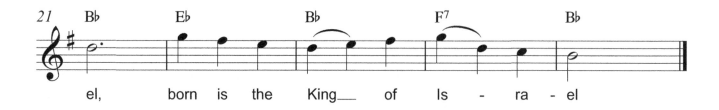

They looked up and saw a star
shining in the east, beyond them far;
and to the earth it gave great light,
and so it continued both day and night.
[Refrain]

And by the light of that same star
three Wise Men came from country far;
to seek for a king was their intent,
and to follow the star wherever it went.
[Refrain]

This star drew nigh to the northwest,
o'er Bethlehem it took its rest;
and there it did both stop and stay,
right over the place where Jesus lay.
[Refrain]

Then entered in those Wise Men three,
full reverently upon the knee,
and offered there, in his presence,
their gold and myrrh and frankincense.
[Refrain]

Once in Royal David's City

Guitar Chords
(standard tuning)

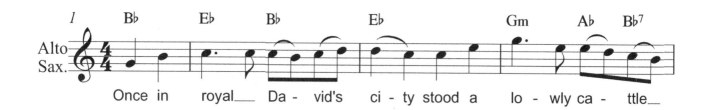

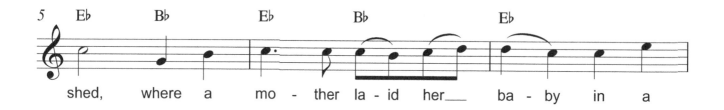

He came down to earth from heaven
who is God and Lord of all;
and his shelter was a stable,
and his cradle was a stall:
with the poor, and meek, and lowly
lived on earth our Savior holy.

Jesus is our childhood's pattern,
day by day like us he grew;
he was little, weak, and helpless,
tears and smiles like us he knew:
and he feels for all our sadness,
and he shares in all our gladness.

And our eyes at last shall see him,
through his own redeeming love,
for that child, so dear and gentle,
is our Lord in heaven above:
and he leads his children on
to the place where he has gone.

Not in that poor lowly stable
with the oxen standing by
we shall see him, but in heaven,
set at God's right hand on high;
there his children gather round,
bright like stars, with glory crowned.

Past Three O'clock

Guitar Chords
(standard tuning)

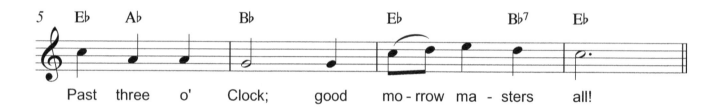

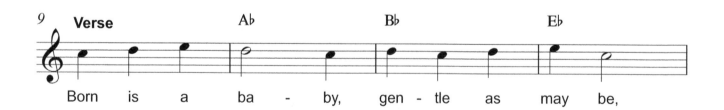

Reprise

Past three o' clock on a cold frosty morning,

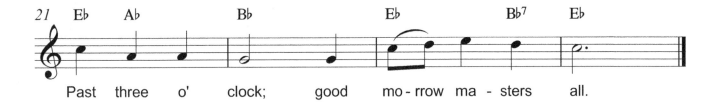

Past three o' clock; good morrow masters all.

Seraph choir singeth,
Angel bell ringeth,
Hark how they rhyme it,
Time it and chime it!
[Reprise]

Mid earth rejoices
Hearing such voices.
Ne'ertofore so well
Carolling nowell!
[Reprise]

Hinds o'er the pearly
Dewy lawn early
Seek the high stranger
Laid in the manager.
[Reprise]

Cheese from the dairy
Bring they for Mary,
And, not for money,
Butter and honey.
[Reprise]

Light out of star-land
Leadeth from far land
Princes, to meet him,
Worship and greet him.
[Reprise]

Myrrh from full coffer,
Incense they offer;
Nor is the golden
Nugget withholden.
[Reprise]

Thus they: I pray you,
Up sirs, nor stay you
Till ye confess him
Likewise and bless him.
[Reprise]

The Holly and the Ivy

Guitar Chords
(standard tuning)

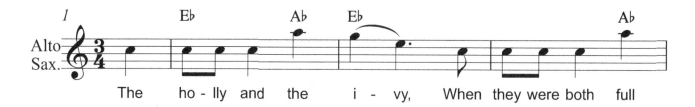

The ho-lly and the i-vy, When they were both full

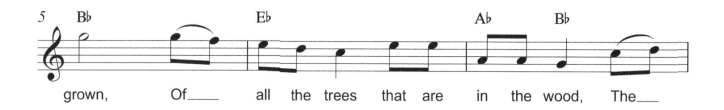

grown, Of___ all the trees that are in the wood, The___

ho-lly bears the crown. The ri-sing of the

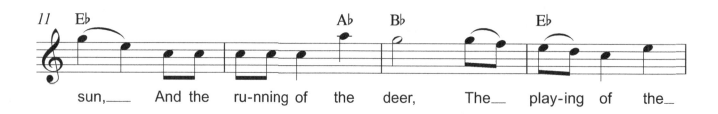

sun,___ And the ru-nning of the deer, The__ play-ing of the__

me-rry or-gan, sweet__ sing-ing in the choir.

The holly bears a blossom,
As white as the lily flower,
And Mary bore sweet Jesus Christ,
To be our sweet Saviour.
[Reprise]

The holly bears a berry,
As red as any blood,
And Mary bore sweet Jesus Christ
For to do us sinners good.
[Reprise]

The holly bears a prickle,
As sharp as any thorn,
And Mary bore sweet Jesus Christ
On Christmas Day in the morn.
[Reprise]

The holly bears a bark,
As bitter as any gall,
And Mary bore sweet Jesus Christ
For to redeem us all.
[Reprise]

The holly and the ivy,
When they are both full grown,
Of all the trees that are in the wood,
The holly bears the crown.
[Reprise[

We Wish You a Merry Christmas

Guitar Chords
(standard tuning)

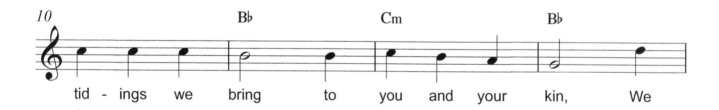

Now bring us some figgy pudding,
Now bring us some figgy pudding,
Now bring us some figgy pudding
And bring it out here.

    Good tidings we bring to you and your kin;
    We wish you a merry Christmas and a happy new year.

For we all like figgy pudding,
For we all like figgy pudding,
For we all like figgy pudding
So bring some out here.

    Good tidings we bring to you and your kin;
    We wish you a merry Christmas and a happy new year.

And we won't go until we've got some,
And we won't go until we've got some,
And we won't go until we've got some
So bring some out here.

    Good tidings we bring to you and your kin;
    We wish you a merry Christmas and a happy new year.

Deck the Halls

Guitar Chords
(standard tuning)

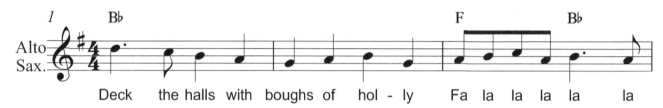

See the flowing bowl before us,
Fa la la la la, la la la la.
Strike the harp and join the chorus.
Fa la la la la, la la la la.

Follow me in merry measure,
Fa la la, la la la, la la la.
While I tell of beauty's teasure,
Fa la la la la, la la la la.

Fast away the old year passes,
Fa la la la la, la la la la.
Hail the new, ye lads and lasses,
Fa la la la la, la la la la.

Laughing, quaffing all together,
Fa la la, la la la, la la la.
Heedless of the wind and weather,
Fa la la la la, la la la la.

In the Bleak Midwinter

Guitar Chords
(standard tuning)

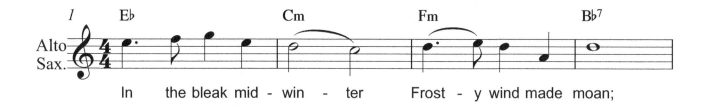

In the bleak mid - win - ter Frost - y wind made moan;

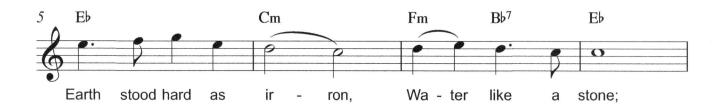

Earth stood hard as ir - ron, Wa - ter like a stone;

Snow had fal - len, snow on snow, snow__ on__ snow,

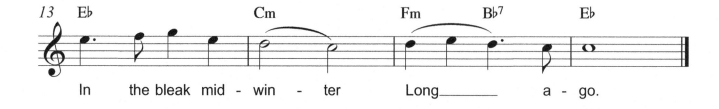

In the bleak mid - win - ter Long_____ a - go.

Our God, heaven cannot hold Him
Nor earth sustain, Heaven and earth shall flee away
When he comes to reign:
In the bleak mid-winter
A stable-place sufficed
The Lord God Almighty -
Jesus Christ.

Enough for Him, whom Cherubim
Worship night and day,
A breastful of milk
And a mangerful of hay;
Enough for Him, whom Angels
Fall down before,
The ox and ass and camel
Which adore.

Angels and Archangels
May have gathere there,
Cherubim and Seraphim
Thronged the air;
But only his Mother
In her maiden bliss
Worshipped the Beloved
With a kiss.

What can I give Him,
Poor as I am? -
If I were a Shepherd
I would bring a lamb;
If I were a Wise Man
I would do my part, -
Yet what can I give Him, -
Give my heart.

Christina Rossetti

Sans Day Carol

Guitar Chords
(standard tuning)

Now the holly bears a berry as green as the grass,
And Mary she bore Jesus, who died on the cross:

Chorus

Now the holly bearsd a berry as black as the coal,
And Mary she bore Jesus, who died for us all:

Chorus

Now the holly bears a berry, as blood is it red,
Then trust we our Saviour, who rose from the dead:

Chorus

Sussex Carol

Guitar Chords
(standard tuning)

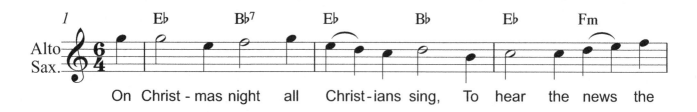

Then why should men on earth be so sad,
Since our Redeemer made us glad,
Then why should men on earth be so sad,
Since our Redeemer made us glad.
When from our sin he set us free,
All for to gain our liberty?

When sin departs before His grace,
Then life and health come in its place.
When sin departs before His grace,
Then life and health come in its place.
Angels and men with joy may sing
All for to see the new born king.

All out of darkness we have light,
Which made the angels sing this night.
All out of darkness we have light,
Which made the angels sing this night:
"Glory to God and peace to men,
Now and for evermore, Amen!"

Gloucestershire Wassail

Refrain

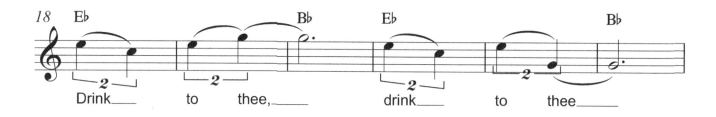

Here's to our horse, and to his right ear,
God send our master a happy new year:
A happy new year as e'er he did see,
With my wassailing bowl I drink to thee.
   Refrain (*sung at the end of each verse*)

So here is to Cherry and to his right cheek
Pray God send our master a good piece of beef
And a good piece of beef that may we all see
With the wassailing bowl, we'll drink to thee.

Here's to our mare, and to her right eye,
God send our mistress a good Christmas pie;
A good Christmas pie as e'er I did see,
With my wassailing bowl I drink to thee.

So here is to Broad Mary and to her broad horn
May God send our master a good crop of corn
And a good crop of corn that may we all see
With the wassailing bowl, we'll drink to thee.

And here is to Fillpail and to her left ear
Pray God send our master a happy New Year
And a happy New Year as e'er he did see
With the wassailing bowl, we'll drink to thee.

Here's to our cow, and to her long tail,
God send our measter us never may fail
Of a cup of good beer: I pray you draw near,
And our jolly wassail it's then you shall hear.

Come butler, come fill us a bowl of the best
Then we hope that your soul in heaven may rest
But if you do draw us a bowl of the small
Then down shall go butler, bowl and all.

Be here any maids? I suppose here be some;
Sure they will not let young men stand on the cold stone!
Sing hey O, maids! come trole back the pin,
And the fairest maid in the house let us all in.

Then here's to the maid in the lily white smock
Who tripped to the door and slipped back the lock
Who tripped to the door and pulled back the pin
 For to let these jolly wassailers in.

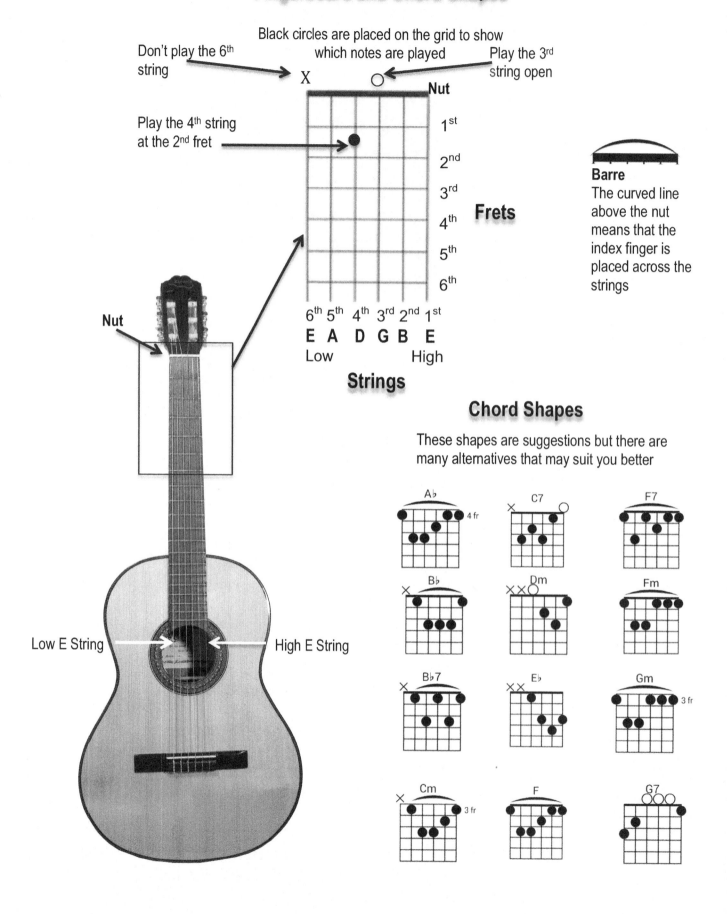

If you have enjoyed **The Wild Music Book of Christmas Carols for Alto Saxophone with Guitar Chords** why not try the other books in the series. Introducing:

Look out for more exciting music coming soon! And many duet combinations with all winds and other instruments
wildmusicpublications.com

@wmpublications

Made in the USA
Middletown, DE
02 November 2022